Defining Excellence

The Discipline of Company Definition

Thomas Metz

Bettencourt

Bettencourt Publishing Ltd.

Published by Bettencourt Publishing Ltd.
Seattle, Washington www.bettencourtpub.com
First edition, 2019

Library of Congress Cataloging-in-Publication Data:

Metz, Thomas V., 1951-
Defining Excellence : The Discipline of Company Definition
/
Thomas V. Metz, Jr.
     p. cm. -- (Bettencourt Finance Series)
     Includes index.
     ISBN-13: 978-0-9898398-3-9
1. Business strategy. 2. Strategic planning. I. Title.

Printed in the United States of America

10 9 8 7 6 5 4 3 2 1

Thomas Metz

Books by Thomas Metz

Selling the Intangible Company:
How to Negotiate and Capture the Value of a Growth Firm

Perfect Your Exit Strategy:
7 Steps to Maximum Value

Why is the United States Rich?
10 Myths Exposed

DEDICATION

With affection, I dedicate this book to my sister,
Mary Elizabeth.

CONTENTS

Thomas Metz

PREFACE

The genesis of this book originated from my work as an investment banker specializing in selling technology companies. Part of the transaction process involves identifying and researching companies that might be good buyers for the company that I was selling.

A consistent theme emerged after a number of years. Companies tended to describe themselves primarily by their technologies and their products. There was little mention of their customers. This left some questions unanswered. Who are they selling to? What is their market?

A business is about much more than just its technology and its products. A business is about customers. The company definitions, however, rarely mentioned the customers.

The management guru Peter Drucker made an important point decades ago about how a company should be defined. Drucker said that a company should be defined by its customers, not by its products or services. I extended Drucker's idea deeper in the customer direction. In my judgment, a business should be defined by the *types of problems* that it solves for its customers.

The book is divided into five parts. The first part delves into company definition and why it matters. It discusses putting the customer at the center and introduces a novel concept called knowledge space.

Part II examines growth strategies, change and the importance of differentiation.

Part III explores the nature of opportunity has well as the enemies of opportunity. It discusses how to create an opportunity strategy and examines the lost art of opportunism.

In Part IV we ponder the business models of the future, the shift to services and the significance of ecosystems and platforms.

Part V presents best practices for creating a first-rate definition. We point out traps to avoid, we critique a number of poor definitions and conclude with 16 rules to construct a great definition.

Defining Excellence

Part I. The Lens of Company Definition

1 THE IMPACT OF COMPANY DEFINITION

A business exists for only one reason—to deliver value to its customers. This is one of the core principles of this book. In essence, a company is a pipeline that provides goods and services to its customers within a knowledge space. Therefore, the company should be defined by its customers, not by its products or services. To be more specific:

A company should be defined by the problems that it solves for its customers.

Stated in a slightly different way—a company should be defined by how it delivers value and to whom.

In the technology industries, most companies define themselves the wrong way. The spotlight is on them, not on the customers. They talk about *their* products and *their* technology and *their* services.

If the purpose of a company is to deliver value to the customer, then the definition of the company should reflect that idea. It should place the primary emphasis on the customers, not on the company's products.

This realization came about in my work as a boutique investment banker researching companies that might be good buyers for the company that my firm is selling. What I noticed was that very few firms defined themselves along the lines of the customer and solving the customer's problem.

In order to identify a good buyer, I want to know what markets they are in, who their customers are and, most importantly, what problems they are solving for their customers. If I could answer these questions, I would have a much better idea if the company was a viable strategic acquirer.

As a company learns about its customers' problems and how to solve these problems, it develops an area of knowledge or a sphere of knowledge. The term that captures it best is "Knowledge Space." Knowledge Space buttresses the company definition and undergirds how the company identifies new areas for growth. We delve deeper into Knowledge Space in Chapter 4.

The Impact on Growth Strategy

How a company defines itself affects how it designs its growth strategy. Just as an individual's self-image defines what a person can or cannot do, how a company defines itself determines what it can or cannot do.

A key point of this book is that growth does not result from asking the question — how can we sell more widgets? My thesis is that if one defines their company by the problems that it solves for its customers, then the company will generate new and different ideas about future opportunities for growth. Many companies define themselves too narrowly, thus the road to growth is too narrow. Recalibrating your company definition is an excellent way to open the door to new areas of opportunity.

2 WHY DEFINITION MATTERS

Why is company definition important? Why does it matter? How you define your company matters because it impacts how you *think* about your company. How a firm defines itself can either broaden or limit the way that it perceives its markets, its customers as well as new growth opportunities.

Company definition matters for five reasons. Company definition:

1. Reinforces how you deliver value
2. Puts the customer at center
3. Improves strategic clarity
4. Is the backbone of strategic planning
5. Provides a bridge to new opportunities

1. Reinforce How You Deliver Value

Recalibrating your company definition can change how you think about your company. What type of company do you want to be in the future? Who are your customers? What competencies and Knowledge Space will you need?

It impacts how you organize your company going forward. With a company definition that is spot on, you will be more effective at creating value, allocating resources and pursuing successful growth strategies.

2. Put the Customer at the Center
A proper company definition puts the customer at the center of the enterprise. The next chapter explores this idea in more depth.

3. Improve Strategic Clarity
Strategic clarity means being clear about who the company serves and how it delivers value. Achieving strategic clarity is difficult.

Everyone agrees, of course, that clear communication is extremely important. Why is it then that so few companies clearly communicate who they are, who they serve and how they deliver value?

Effective communication fosters better relationships with customers, employees, future customers and with the world at large. Most importantly, communication is how you connect effectively with your customers.

Effective company definition is really about truth. Truth is related to trust. Effective communication improves trust and trust is imperative for any business for building good relationships with its customers.

4. The Backbone for Strategic Planning
Company definition is the backbone of strategic planning; it underpins your growth strategy. In preparing this section, I researched the top ten

management consulting firms to discover their perspectives on strategic planning. Just like company definitions, there were a lot of buzzwords, fancy phrases and some meaningless drivel.

Several of the consulting firms articulated ideas about strategic planning that are the polar opposite of defining a business by the problem that it solves for the customer. The wrong way to think about strategic planning is to focus internally, analyze strengths and weaknesses and ask questions about allocating resources. Several firms discussed competitive

> One strategic planning practice that stood out positively was Bain & Company, the Boston-based consulting firm. Bain defines strategic planning quite well. It states: "Strategic planning is a comprehensive process for determining what a business should become and how it can best achieve that goal." It goes on to state, "It appraises the full potential of a business and explicitly links the business's objectives to the actions and resources required to achieve them." ("Strategic Planning." 2 April 2018, www.bain.com/insights/management-tools-strategic-planning.)
>
> These two sentences just nail it. Bain's comment about "what a business should become" is another way of posing the question—who should our customers be and how should we deliver value to them? Later in the description, Bain talks about "target potential business arenas and explore each market for emerging threats and opportunities." This is good because it focuses the company's strategic planning on customers and on the future.

advantage and differentiation. Differentiation is an important concept; however, strategic planning should focus on the customer's problems before considering differentiation.

5. Bridge to Growth Opportunities
When you do come across market opportunities, how will you know which ones to choose? A clear company definition will help you determine what new products to add, what services to develop and which acquisitions to make.

An effective growth strategy must be based on a distinct and accurate company definition. With a proper company definition, a company may view its tangential markets in a new light. You will see your growth path differently. You will appreciate opportunities differently.

The next chapter delves into the concept of putting the customer at the center of your business. Many firms talk about the importance of the customer but often these are just empty words. This is particularly true in the technology sectors. Serving the customer is every business's reason for existence.

3 PUT THE CUSTOMER AT THE CENTER

Technology will eventually become obsolete,
but customers will always have needs.

Put the customer at the center of your enterprise. Becoming customer-centric is not a strategy; it is an orientation. It changes the way that you do things. It is an organizing paradigm.

If you define your company by the problems that you solve for the customer, everything else will flow from there. You will view your business as an entity whose sole purpose delivering value to the customers. Your raison d'être is not to be a technology company or a widget manufacturer. It is simply to deliver value to your customers and figure out the best way to solve their problems.

As Amazon's Jeff Bezos elegantly stated:

> *"We start with the customer and we work backward... Rather than to ask what are we good at and what else can we do with that skill, you ask who are our customers? What do they need? And then you say were going to give that to them regardless of whether we currently have the skills to do so, and we will learn those skills no matter how long it takes. The Kindle is a good example... We had to acquire new skills."*
> (Daniel Lyons, "Jeff Bezos," *Newsweek*, Jan. 4, 2010, p. 85)

This is the essence of being customer centric.

A business exists solely to serve its customers. So, organize your business around the customer. This raises the obvious question — what does it mean to put the customer at the center of your enterprise?

The phrase "Get close to the customer" is hackneyed but it is right on the money. What does it mean to get close to the customer? It means to see the world through the customer's eyes. It means understanding their issues and problems. It means knowing where they want to go and helping them achieve their goals. Build a relationship with each of your customers. You must truly believe that the customer comes first.

Customers want to know that you understand them. They want to know that you appreciate what their problems are and what they are trying to achieve. They want to know that you can help them, that you will be there for them. Too many organizations give lip service to being "customer centric" but they do not actually put the customer at the center of the enterprise.

The follow-on question is — what new problems might our customers have in the future? How can we help them with these problems? If we do not currently have the skill set to solve these problems, then we must develop or acquire those skills.

Many companies ponder how they can better utilize their current skills and competencies and how can they sell into additional markets. In other words, they are asking the question: "How can we sell more widgets?"

This is the wrong question. Completely the wrong question. The right question is, "Who are our customers and what problems can we solve for them? The savvy business will view itself as a solver of customer problems not simply as a maker of products.

Successful companies realize that they are really in the customer-experience business. Give customers what they really want — not more products or services, but meaningful outcomes. It is no longer about selling things; it's about delivering results.

A meaningful outcome means that the customer's need has been satisfied. These words actually mean something. It is about *outcomes*.

Do not let competition drive your strategy. Focus on your customers, not on the competition. This means that the customer is at the core of your strategy, not your competitors. Too many companies let competition drive their strategies. You are not there to beat your competitors; you are there to serve your customers.

A business must build a strong feedback loop with its customers. Get feedback in order to drive continuous improvement. Develop success metrics that are genuinely based on the customer. That way you can serve their needs earlier and better. You can keep ahead of change.

Perhaps you should focus on people and companies that are *not* your customers and ask — how can we make them our customers? To create *new* demand an organization needs to focus to noncustomers. Enter a new sector. Create new niche markets. Get new types of customers. What are their needs?

A truly customer-centric business will have a long-term orientation. To succeed over the long term, you must keep your customers happy and satisfied. Companies need to understand their customers across the entire lifecycle. Customer lifetime value is an excellent concept. This promotes a long-term orientation.

Reframing is the First Step

Reframing your company definition is the first step to becoming a truly customer-centric company. Figure out what the customer wants and needs, then develop products and services based upon those areas.

In the technology markets it is even more important to focus on the customer. It is too easy for companies to get sidetracked by their cool technology, their cool products and take their eye off the ball. By taking their eye off the ball, I mean forgetting to put the customer first. Technologies will always become obsolete, but customers will always have needs.

What a company knows about its customers, about their problems, their issues and their objectives has an important influence on a company's strategy for delivering value going forward. Knowledge about customer problems and how to solve them is what I characterize as Knowledge Space. A company's definition is impacted by its Knowledge Space and we examine this concept in the next chapter.

4 APPRECIATE YOUR KNOWLEDGE SPACE

What do you know about your customers?

K nowledge Space is the area around which a company has expertise, knowledge and credibility. A Knowledge Space embodies the awareness that a business has about its customers and the customers' problems. The business delivers products and services to customers within this space. This is the knowledge embodied in your company and its people. Knowledge Space undergirds how a company creates and delivers value.

A company develops credibility around a Knowledge Space. Customers develop trust for the company within this space. In addition, Knowledge Space shapes how companies grow and where they explore for opportunities.

Knowledge Space differs from core competency. Core competencies refer to a set of skills whereas Knowledge Space refers to an area of knowledge. Knowledge Space is a broader concept than core competency. Core competency represents an *internal* focus. It depicts the company and its skills and abilities. Knowledge Space represents an *external* focus. It encompasses the intelligence that the company has about a market sector and the needs of customers. It embodies what the company understands.

Core competencies refer to skills, techniques and abilities that a company can perform. Core competencies imply the capability to do something or to produce something. Certainly, one must have knowledge in order to have the skills, but it is a narrower connotation.

Apple's core competency is design. One of Amazon's core competencies is logistics and shipping. Nike's core competency is marketing.

Competence means you can *do* something. Knowledge Space means that you *know* something.

Monetize Your Knowledge Space

A company can monetize its Knowledge Space by turning its knowledge into new products and new services. Let's consider one good illustration.

The Square Example

Have you ever bought a piece of art at a neighborhood fair or some maple syrup at a farmer's market and paid with your credit card? Square probably handled the credit card transaction. Square is a small card swiper that plugs into a smart phone or an iPad.

Square has gotten to know its merchant customers very well. As a result, it now it offers cash advances and small loans that banks would not make. Loans vary in size and the average is $6,000. This is a very beneficial service for these small merchants. This division of Square is named Square Capital. In the first three years, Square Capital extended $1.8 billion in funds to small merchants. This example underscores the idea of utilizing the company's Knowledge Space to move into new areas of opportunity.

What is Square's Knowledge Space? It is understanding small merchants and their financial needs. Square understands these businesses because it has been handling their financial transactions. It knows their transaction volume and it knows if there are repeat customers, which is helpful when making loans.

Square got the idea by listening to feedback from its customers. These small businesses could not get normal bank loans and Square recognized this as an opportunity. So, it moved into the lending business.

Square's original competency was processing credit card transactions, not making loans. Now the company has developed a new competency — lending money to small merchants. Square is a good example of a company that successfully monetized its Knowledge Space.

Many businesses consider their Knowledge Space too narrowly; thus, the path to growth is too narrow. These companies need to re-evaluate their Knowledge Space in order to open up the company to new kinds of growth possibilities.

Thomas Metz

Part II. The Growth Imperative

5 GROWTH REQUIRES CHANGE

The entrepreneur always searches for change, responds to it, and exploits it as an opportunity.

— Peter Drucker
(*Innovation and Entrepreneurship*, New York: Harper & Row, 1985.)

Growth is the essential element for creating shareholder value. Initiatives associated with growing revenue drive more value than any other action. Growth is more important than cost structures or margins. It is better to get revenues up than costs down. Higher growth drives a greater market capitalization and is the key predictor of success over the long term.

Many factors can constrain a company's growth. The industry may be mature. The technology may be old, on the wrong platform or the products are outdated. A company may lack the sales and marketing resources to effectively address the market. Long sales cycles can be a considerable challenge for smaller companies. The lack of financial resources can limit progress. People issues and organizational problems can also constrain growth.

Sometimes companies have several of these problems — which is really a killer. If that is the case, the best course of action may be to find a strategic acquirer and sell the business.

Where are the high growth sectors? You may need to develop or acquire new products, new services and new capabilities. Find ways to differentiate. Differentiation is a key driver of long-term growth.

Have the fortitude to move into a new sector. Explore the tangential and adjacent markets with an open mind. Who are the players there? What differentiates them? Every market has adjacent markets; therefore, there are always opportunities.

When you push the boundaries, there is always an advantage. Look for movement. How can you deliver more value? Think outside the box. Seek opportunity at the edges.

A business that is open to change is a business that will respond to the shifting needs of its customers. As customers grow their needs will change. The smart business will grow and change as its customers grow and change.

It is not the strongest of the species that survives, not the most intelligent that survives. It is the one that is the most adaptable to change.

— Charles Darwin

This quote by Darwin captures the importance of change. A business that wants to grow is a business that must make changes. It must change its approach to the market, change its products and services or change something else, but it must make changes.

Change what? Change the way that you think about your company. Change the way that you view your markets. Change how you deliver value to your customers. Change how you consider new sources of revenue and new growth opportunities. Most importantly, change the way that you think about and define your company.

Change is uncomfortable. Change means facing uncertainty. It is scary. It can open you up to failure. On the positive side, the more things change, the more opportunities there are.

Always Change a Losing Game

If you want to succeed, it is critical to change a losing game. This is certainly true in sports, but it is also true in business.

If you will permit a tennis analogy, I learned this lesson the hard way. I used to play competitive tennis. If I was losing, I thought if I simply executed better, the match would turn around. In other words, hit the same shots but be more accurate and make fewer errors. Stick with the same plan but try harder. I was wrong. Being a stubborn person, it took me quite some time to learn this lesson the hard way.

Eventually I realized that I had to change my strategy. If I did not, I would lose. Don't try to hit the same shots better. Mix it up. Change the speed of the shots...hit some hard and some soft. Utilize more spin. Use different types of spin. Perhaps throw in a few drop shots. Come to the net more often. Do something different to keep him or her off balance. Mix it up. It is imperative to change a losing game.

There are a multitude of ways to change a losing game in business. Develop or acquire new products. Create new value-added services. Change the way you sell, perhaps move to a direct sales model. Arrange new partnerships that could generate additional sales. Divest a product line. Outsource some of your operations. This list could continue, but you get the idea. If things are not going well, you must make changes.

We wrap up this section with an old maxim.

"If you do not change direction, you may end up where you are heading."

— Lao Tzu

Now, Lao was not really a business guy (or a tennis player), so he does not have any particular credibility in this arena. However, it is difficult to argue with his point.

Companies must change the way that they think about their businesses. This leads to the key message of this book—change the way that you define your company.

A business must make changes in order to open the

door to new opportunities. Opportunity will not come knocking on your door. It starts with making changes.

Thomas Metz

6 FIRE-UP YOUR GROWTH STRATEGY

Agrowth strategy is about where you want to go. The strategy includes several elements. It articulates what markets and customers you want to serve in the future and what problems you want to solve for your customers. Let's consider some important questions. The obvious question is—what should our growth strategy be? This seems like the right question; however, it is not actionable or focused. A better question is—how should we create and deliver value to our customers? A follow-up question is—who should our customers be in the future?

A growth strategy involves reviewing your business model to see where you need to make adjustments or perhaps, even major changes. It includes seeking out new opportunities.

Our economy is becoming increasingly sophisticated. Customers do not simply want widgets anymore. They want widget services, widget maintenance, updating of the latest widget, or a widget app and they want the widget connected to the other parts of their lives or businesses.

They may prefer to rent or lease your widgets, rather than purchase your widgets. They might choose to pay an annual fee to have your widget service available to them.

If your company does not provide these ancillary services, you will eventually be left behind because your competitors will provide these services. The reason that competitors will offer them is because there is opportunity in doing so. Opportunity exists because the full widget service makes it much easier for customers to solve their widget problems. Easier is always better.

As our economy continues to become more sophisticated and more connected, the last thing people want is a partial solution. They want the complete solution. A product-focused strategy is not sustainable over the long run.

Another consequence of a sophisticated economy is that companies are selling more services and fewer standalone products. This is where the growth occurs — providing new services that deliver value to the customer. Chapter 11 discusses the shift to services in more depth.

Give customers what they really want — not more products, but more meaningful outcomes. Business is no longer about selling things — it's about selling results. What customers really want is results.

MASTER THE LONG GAME

A short-term plan addresses how to sell more products. But in the long run you will need a different strategy. Stay close to your customer, understand your customers and solve their problems. Master the long game.

There are two ways to extend a business. The first is to recognize what you are good at, your skills and competencies, and ask what else you can do with those abilities. This has been the traditional path to formulating a growth strategy.

This book has a different thesis. In this book we are focusing on identifying and solving customer problems, not simply pursuing where we can sell more of our products.

The second way asks the question—who are your customers and what do they need? Then work backwards to develop the skills and resources so you can solve your customers' problems. This approach is more powerful over the long term. It also ensures that you will always have customers.

MOVE INTO ADJACENT MARKETS

The most obvious potential new markets are the markets that are adjacent to your current markets. Moving into adjacent markets is a great way to generate new growth opportunities.

Adjacent to Whom?

Not so fast. What do you consider an adjacent market? A critical point is how one defines "adjacent." An adjacent market is not called that because it is adjacent to the company, but because it is adjacent to the *customer*. This is an important delineation.

One of the fundamental tenets of this book is to view markets through the eyes of the customer. This is true for adjacent markets as well. In other words, a market is termed adjacent because it is adjacent to the customer, not because it is adjacent to the company. It is a very different orientation.

The best way to describe moving into adjacent markets is through several examples.

Tesla Insures

Tesla, the electric car company, plans to create and sell its own car insurance. The idea is that the insurance should cost less because Tesla has better safety benefits than most other cars. Tesla's crash avoidance features reduce claims for injury liability and for physical damage. Tesla claims to have extensive data about the safety performance of its vehicles.

Since every Tesla car is connected to the Internet at all times, it is fairly straightforward to monitor driver behavior. Certainly not everyone will want this, but for careful drivers this could lead to better insurance rates.

Although still in the early stages, this is an excellent example of a company developing new products for its existing customer base.

Zillow Flips

Zillow Group recently made an interesting move into adjacent markets. The online real estate company now purchases homes directly with cash. It launched this business in Phoenix and Las Vegas and is expanding into additional markets across the U.S. It renovates the homes and resells them. Zillow takes much of the uncertainty out of the sale process; there are no showings or open houses and the closing date is certain. Some sellers value convenience and timing more than price. Zillow purchases only about 4% of the homes that sellers offer to it. The company purchased 900 homes in the first quarter of 2019 and it is expanding into 20 additional markets. Eventually, Zillow may expand into ancillary services such as title insurance and mortgages.

We Work Invests

WeWork is an excellent example of a company making a shift. WeWork rents out flexible office space to startups, freelancers and small businesses. It provides various office services as well as a sense of community. It recently launched a venture capital fund. With its new venture fund, WeWork makes investments in young companies that were already its customers. In addition, WeWork has made a few additional of these so-called "shift acquisitions." One of these was the acquisition of Meetup, the organizing platform.

In each of these examples, customer need is the common denominator, not the product or service. These companies are not asking how they can we sell more cars, more real estate ads or rent more office space. They are asking—what additional services can we provide to our current customers? That is the better question.

Sometimes adjacent markets are only thought of as adjacent in retrospect. If Square defined itself narrowly—as a payment processing company, it never would have gone into the lending business. The lesson here is to be creative and resourceful in how you view adjacent markets.

WORK BACKWARDS

Determine what your customers need and work

backwards to figure out how to serve these needs. This may require developing or acquiring new skills.

The quote by Amazon's Jeff Bezos in Chapter 3 nicely describes the strategy of working backwards to serve the customer. Bezos was referring to the Kindle. In the early days of Amazon, its customers were readers of books. Amazon did not invent technical products; it just sold stuff on the Internet. But Bezos wanted to better serve its customers who were readers. Given advances in technology, Bezos thought there must be a way to invent a simple reader, or reading machine, kind of like a smart phone but bigger. So, Amazon put together a hardware engineering team to design and build the Kindle. They had to acquire new skills to get the job done. In retrospect, of course, the Kindle and e-books have been a major success for Amazon.

How can you develop the resources and capabilities to serve a new customer need? First of all, you can train your employees or hire people that have the required skills. Secondly, your firm could acquire another company that already possesses these skills.

The fundamental point is to take a different tack; identify a customer need and then work backwards to develop the skills and resources to address that need.

As you develop your growth strategy, you should also reevaluate your business model. A business model describes how a company creates and delivers value. It defines the value proposition and describes how the company organizes itself in order to produce value.

New technologies produce new products and services. New technologies also change the way that products and services are delivered. Thus, the nature of the market changes. When the market changes, a company must modify its business model. More and more companies are discovering that they are part of business ecosystems. An ecosystem connects companies and products and services to the customer. It may be a good idea to reevaluate your business model with respect to the new ecosystems. As the company solves new and different types of customer problems, the business model will change. As the business model changes, it is likely that the company will need to change the way that it defines itself. We delve into business models of the future in Part IV.

Develop New Opportunities
Developing new opportunities is an essential part of your growth strategy. This strategy should include two types of actions. The first is a targeted search that seeks specific products or services to add. The second action is an exploration for new varieties of opportunities. This second aspect is the most interesting and we examine it in depth in Chapter 10.

How do you solve customers' problems differently than your competitors? How do you add value in ways that your competitors do not? The next chapter delves into the benefits of differentiation.

Thomas Metz

7 DIFFERENTIATE FOR SUSTAINED GROWTH

Differentiation is the only path to sustained growth. Differentiation drives the business model. You must have complete clarity about your strategic differentiation.

One of the first rules of marketing is — don't tell them why you are good; tell them how you are different. This is also true for your strategy and for your company definition.

Figure out what truly differentiates you from your competitors. Why do customers choose your company rather than a competitor? What is your strongest strategic advantage? What sets you apart? Make sure the answers to these questions are based on facts not on wishes or beliefs.

If your company is similar to your competitors, then no one really needs you. It is because you add value in a different way that you have an advantage. Recalibrate your company definition so it differentiates your business.

What are your sources of differentiation? It is lower prices? Higher-quality? Faster service? A combination of these? Differentiation can be as simple as superior execution. It does not need to be gimmicks or catchy slogans.

Innovation is a great way to achieve differentiation. Apple, for example, is extremely good at innovating. Reputation can also be an excellent differentiating factor. The more you can differentiate, the more value you can deliver and the greater your advantage.

Your Knowledge Space can impact your differentiation as well. Your firm may have accumulated unique knowledge over the years that competitors do not have.

Typically, a company will achieve differentiation and enjoy initial success. Competitors, however, may copy the differentiating factors of the successful companies. As you move forward, you must continually adjust and modify your differentiation to stay ahead of your competitors. Build strong feedback loops with your customers.

The successful companies are the most highly differentiated. These companies build relentlessly on their differentiating factors and they sustain their differentiation over the long term.

Now we are going to shift gears and take a new road in the direction of opportunity. The first step is to ponder the true nature of opportunity.

Part III. Opportunity

8 THE NATURE OF OPPORTUNITY

*An opportunity exists only when you can see it
and it will be seen only if it is looked for.
Opportunities are created, they are not found.*

This chapter explores several important questions about opportunity: What is the nature of opportunity? Where do opportunities reside? How should we seek opportunities?

The opposite of opportunity-seeking is neither steady growth nor safety — it is inertia and atrophy. Opportunities can cause disruption, risk and aggravation. You must embrace them anyway.

Most companies think that they are open to opportunities, but in reality, they are not. They may be "keeping their eyes open," but keeping one's eyes open does not create opportunity. Opportunities must be deliberately pursued in order to be created and developed. The smart company cannot afford *not* to aggressively seek opportunities.

The Context of the Beholder

Opportunities are hard to spot because they don't look like opportunities. Opportunity is not a function of the external world or the market. It is a function of one's knowledge, competence and one's interaction with the markets. It is the confluence of a knowledge set and a market situation.

Opportunities are not self-evident. An opportunity is not like a $100 bill lying on the sidewalk to be found by the first passerby. "Hello there, I am an opportunity!" No, they do not come nicely labeled.

Opportunities are subjective; they are not objective. An opportunity exists in the mind of the beholder; it does not exist solely by itself. An opportunity for one person or company may not be an opportunity for another person or company.

One must have a context or a point of view in order to recognize opportunity. For example, a mechanic views a broken-down car for sale as an opportunity. The mechanic can buy the car, fix it up and sell it for a gain. The car represents an opportunity for the mechanic. For someone who does not know how to repair cars, this is not an opportunity. Thus, the opportunity depends on the knowledge and capabilities of the seeker.

Apple Computer moved into the telephone business quite successfully. The mobile phone market was expanding rapidly. Any number of companies could have developed a better mobile telephone. However,

Apple did it and they did it more successfully than any other firm. Apple succeeded because it combined the market need for a better telephone with their incredible product design capabilities. Without their design capabilities, this would not be an opportunity for Apple. The opportunity was the market situation combined with Apple's knowledge and competencies.

WHERE DOES OPPORTUNITY RESIDE?

Opportunities can be developed and created in a number of places. They are created at the edges of market boundaries and in the interstices. Opportunities are discovered when there is turmoil and uncertainty. Constraints and hardship hold the seeds of opportunity because through hardship we see things differently. Movement creates opportunity and failure can give rise to opportunities.

The Edges

Look at the edges — the edges of the market, the edges of a geographic area, the edges of anything. Most people do not look at the edges, they look at the middle. The middle has already been discovered. There is no opportunity in the middle. The edge is where opportunity resides.

Interstices

Look for the interstices, the places in between. The more interstices there are, the more opportunities there are. In today's complex world there are more interstices than ever before.

Movement

Movement creates opportunity. It does so because

37

movement changes things. A movement away from one area is a movement towards something else, even if the something else has yet to be discovered. Look for the movement away from the middle, the movement toward the edges.

Turmoil

Wherever there is turmoil, there is indecision. And where there is indecision, there is opportunity. The savvy business can profit from disarray in the markets. As Einstein said, "In the middle of difficulty lies opportunity." Volatility also produces opportunity. Turbulence is your friend.

Constraints

Constraints are a source of opportunity. They are similar to hardships. Constraints and hardships cause us to view things differently. And viewing things differently is the first step to recognizing an area of opportunity.

Uncertainty

The more uncertainty there is in a particular area, the more opportunity exists there. Uncertainty is a key component of opportunity and more opportunities exist in uncertain times. If there is no uncertainty, there is no opportunity.

The nature of opportunity is such that there are opportunities in many places at all times.

THE MIND OF THE SEEKER

The seeker of opportunities possesses a restless intelligence and an open-ended sense of discovery. He is flexible. On one hand the seeker has a strong sense of reality. On the other hand, he believes that reality can change. A seeker takes a fresh look from the outside. He or she is similar to a jazz musician. Classical music is played the same way every time; jazz is interpreted and played differently each time. The seeker hears resonance in the market; he varies the timbre of the idea.

Opportunities are not discovered by keeping an eye open. An opportunity materializes only when it can be recognized and it can be recognized only if one is deliberately looking for it. It takes purposeful creative effort to identify opportunity. To find opportunity one must actively seek out opportunity. Opportunity will not find you.

It is human nature to connect dots and perceive patterns. Disconnecting the old dots can be illuminating. Ignore some of the dots or invent new dots and see what patterns emerge. The first step in creating new patterns is to disconnect the old dots.

A seeker of opportunity tries to discover unexpected patterns. The critical word is "unexpected." An expectation limits one's vision. One must rid oneself of expectations in order to free up the mind.

Sometimes it is easier to spot other peoples' opportunities than your own opportunities. Perceiving unexpected patterns is illustrated by the game of Boggle—looking for words on a grid of lettered dice. Rather than trying to force a preconceived word, let the words come to you. That is the mind of the seeker.

The role of the seeker is to perceive, not to analyze. Analytical skills are not in short supply. Perception, however, is a different story. The ability to perceive new ways of doing things, perceive new types of relationships, perceive new service ideas and new niches is an uncommon talent. Perception is more important than analysis.

Opportunity search is a process of exploration and discovery. The seeker of opportunity simply goes exploring. The seeker sees in non-traditional ways. It is a nonlinear exercise. The seeker goes into an idea from the side door. He sneaks up on it.

To develop new opportunities, a company can't simply keep its eyes open, it must pursue opportunities aggressively.

We close out this chapter with two noteworthy notions from the thinker, Edward de Bono.

The opposite of opportunity seeking is not stability or conservatism, it is stagnation and atrophy.

Sometimes an obvious route only becomes obvious after we have found it — and we wonder why we did not spot it in the first place.

(de Bono, Edward. *Opportunities.* Penguin Books, 1978)

9 ENEMIES OF OPPORTUNITY

Many traditional business practices impede the discovery of opportunities. Businesses have strategic plans, analytical processes, criteria, committees and an emphasis on focus. Even a successful business model can constrict opportunity seeking. Why are these practices the enemies of opportunity?

Strategic Planning
Strategic planning is about saying "We want to go there. Let's make a plan to get there." Opportunity seeking is an open-ended exploration; it is the exact opposite of planning.

Focus
Focus implies a narrowing of concentration. Opportunity seeking involves a broader view, looking outward.

Analysis
The analytical mindset is the antithesis of

opportunity. Analyzing concentrates on what is already there; it does not discover the new.

Quantification
A manager's demand for quantification can hinder finding opportunity. Opportunities are usually qualitative in nature.

More Data
Collecting more data does not eliminate the need for ideas. Data does not create opportunities.

Committees
Committees are not effective at identifying opportunities. Fear of judgment by a peer or a supervisor inhibits one from expressing unusual ideas that can lead to opportunities.

Questions
Sometimes questions can be the enemy of opportunity, such as "what is your rationale?" In opportunity seeking, there is no rationale; we are just exploring.

Successful Business Models
Successful business models can encourage a business to continue doing things the same way when perhaps they should be doing things in new ways.

Modern businesses have many built-in biases against the discovery of opportunity. How many times have we heard the statement "that market is too small," or "that acquisition is too small?" This is not opportunistic thinking. This is taking the safe road. This is looking backwards. All large markets were small markets at one time. All large companies were once small companies. Most management teams are skilled at strategic planning; however, few are proficient at developing a genuine opportunity strategy. Business people are taught to analyze and solve problems, not to discover opportunity. Creating opportunities is an entirely different skill set.

Now that we have a clear idea about the nature opportunities and the enemies of opportunities, how can we develop a plan to generate new opportunities? The next chapter explores the concept of creating an opportunity strategy. It may be different than you think.

Thomas Metz

10 CRAFT AN OPPORTUNITY STRATEGY

The problem is that the world changes out from under you if you do not develop new competencies and push into new markets. That is why you must explore — to keep fresh, to keep moving, find new problems to solve, to gain new skills and to keep looking for attractive new sectors.

Your strategy for identifying and developing new opportunities is a key driver of growth. How you think about and define your company impacts how you consider new areas of opportunity. Keeping your eyes open is not a strategy.

To create an effective opportunity strategy, consider three stratagems:

- Go for a walk in the market
- Test the edges
- Be opportunistic

GO FOR A WALK IN THE MARKET

Sometimes it is a good idea to go down uncharted alleys and see what's at the end. Many times these are dead ends, but sometimes they open up to broad avenues and exciting new markets.

An important distinction must be made between an exploration and a targeted search. A targeted search seeks *specific* products, technologies or acquisitions that the company is looking for. An example would be filling a gap in a product line. This is not a new concept; companies have been undertaking targeted searches for decades.

Exploring is different. It is opportunistic. A company is not seeking anything specific, it is simply going out for a walk in the market. This is not a path that many firms take.

Go for a stroll in the market and see what is happening out there. Do you notice anything that you can take advantage of? Who are the players? Who is doing what? What problems are they solving for their customers? Do these needs or solutions intersect with your company?

How does exploring actually work? The search process that I employ when selling a company is very similar to a company exploring for growth opportunities. The only difference is that I am representing the selling company. The process is exactly the same. I go out for a stroll in the market to see what I can discover.

When searching for potential buyers, there are always the known companies in the primary market; these are the obvious candidates. There are no surprises there. Plus, there are always a few adjacent markets that are also no-brainers; in other words, they are fairly obvious as well.

The exploring really starts when I begin examining the markets sectors that are not obvious. These sectors are tangential or remotely adjacent to the main market. In many cases, they are only obliquely adjacent.

The company that I am representing will be a strategic acquisition for the buyer and many times it is not on the buyer's radar. I am presenting them with a new type of opportunity. The company being acquired might be a new product line, a new service, a new division or new technology that the buyer can incorporate.

Exploring is a process of discovery. When you go exploring, you run across things that you never would have thought of. It can lead to serendipity. There are surprises and, many times, opportunities.

You may discover a company that is solving a new type of customer problem that you were unaware of. This need may be an opportunity for your company.

TEST THE EDGES

Meaningful change always occurs at the edges. The world is driven by what happens at the margins.

Testing the edges is a great way to push on the market and generate opportunities. Every market touches on a number of tangential markets. This is where new ideas emerge. There are always adjacent markets; thus, there are always opportunities.

Many small companies are solving new and interesting problems that the big companies are not addressing. These are small markets that may develop into large markets. Many of these markets offer excellent opportunities for growth.

Market boundaries are not a given; they can be reshaped. Do not get locked into existing industry structures. Expand your horizons. Push the boundaries and seek opportunity at the edges.

Bold Moves

Sometimes companies need to make bold moves to generate growth; take new actions that are out of the ordinary. Take a risk.

A good example of a company that needed to make some of bold moves is Avis. The car rental company had been struggling in recent years. The rental car market was mature, profits had slowed and the stock price was down. Plus, competitors like Lyft and Uber had impacted the business.

Avis made several bold moves in the last few years. They acquired Zipcar, the self-serve company that rents cars on an hourly basis. Avis also began renting cars to Lyft drivers. The company partnered with Waymo to manage Waymo's fleet of self-driving cars. Avis is investing heavily in new technology to connect its fleet of cars to the Internet, to shorten wait times and manage vehicle maintenance activities.

The company deserves credit for making these bold moves. If Avis defined its company by the statement "we just rent cars" then it would not have undertaken these new initiatives.

Another example of testing the edge and redrawing market boundaries is Office Depot's acquisition of CompuCom Systems. The office products market had been growing very slowly, only about 1% annually. Office Depot needed to make some changes to get back on the road to growth.

Why did it acquire CompuCom? Because the

customer bases overlapped to a large degree. CompuCom employs 6,000 technicians who provide technology support. These IT support services include remote help desk, data centers and onsite support. CompuCom will serve as Office Depot's technology services platform. Now Office Depot can offer new value-added services to the same set of business customers. This acquisition was a good first step in Office Depot's transformation to redefine itself and become a broader technology services company.

Testing the edges and making bold moves are excellent tactics to produce new growth opportunities. Another way to trigger new growth possibilities is opportunism.

THE LOST ART OF OPPORTUNISM

To be opportunistic means to take advantage of circumstances. Opportunism is the opposite of planning.

If your company has a plenty of new projects in the works and opportunities to choose from, you probably do not need to make opportunistic moves. However, if your growth has tapered off, if you are a little bit "stuck," you should consider taking opportunistic actions. When your road to growth is narrow, it's time to make some changes.

In the technology world, CEOs and managers are rarely opportunistic. For them it is all about focus, focus, focus. They focus on their technology and on their products. They focus on the new version of the technology and the next product release.

It is difficult to criticize focus. Focus seems like you know what you are doing. You have a specific purpose and a goal or objective in mind. If a manager is highly focused on developing his or her unique technology and it doesn't work out, it doesn't look so bad. If it fails, well, at least they were very focused. They tried hard.

On the other hand, it is easy to be criticized for pursuing an opportunistic endeavor if it doesn't work out. There is risk in making opportunistic moves or an opportunistic acquisition of a company or a product line. If it does not work out, the manager could be open to serious criticism. What were you thinking? You did not have a well-defined strategy?

A CEO can't just have his head down focusing all the time. He or she must pay attention to the world, to the markets and continually seek new opportunities for growth.

There are three fundamental types of opportunism:

(1) *Know How to Solve.* Sometimes a business will uncover a customer need and it is fairly sure that it has the tools and knowledge to solve that issue. (In other words, it is within your skill set and knowledge space.)

(2) *Have Some Idea.* A company has some appreciation for the customer problem and how to go about solving it, but it is only partially figured out. (Your knowledge space overlaps to some degree.)

(3) *No Solution Yet.* A firm notices the customer need but it does not actually have the knowledge or resources to solve that problem. To take advantage of this opportunity it must obtain the necessary skills to solve the problem. (It is not part of your current knowledge space.)

Opportunism requires action. You cannot "see" an opportunity. All you can see is something that might be an opportunity. Whether it truly is an opportunity or not depends on the action taken and the success of that action.

The opportunity only becomes real once it has been acted upon. It is this process of acting on it that makes the opportunity a reality.

If an entrepreneur acts on what he believes is an opportunity and it fails, was that really an opportunity? Perhaps the action was ineffective. Hard to tell. What is the difference? Should he or she try again? Try a new angle, try a different strategy?

Remember that every opportunity is a customer problem or a customer need. The business may or may not have an effective solution for that problem but the need is there nevertheless.

Being opportunistic requires a strategy that is fluid. There are two types of strategies—fixed strategies and fluid strategies. Most strategies are fixed strategies. A company utilizes a fixed strategy when it knows the needs of the market.

Most companies love a good strategic plan. It is difficult to argue with a CEO, vice president or committee that puts forth a well-articulated strategic plan. The plan may be right or it may be wrong, but it usually sounds pretty good. There are reasons, typically good reasons, that support the plan. These are fixed strategies.

A fluid strategy is different. A fluid strategy is utilized when there is uncertainty about the market and about the customers' need. It is the opposite of a fixed strategy. There may be uncertainty about the best ways to solve the customer problem. The fluid strategy embraces this uncertainty.

With a fluid strategy, you explore and see where it goes. Try a few experiments. Take some actions and see if you can make progress on solving the customer's problem. You respond to nuances in the marketplace. If certain tactics don't work, you adjust and try different tactics. That is the essence of a fluid strategy. Executing a fluid strategy is what creates new markets.

Markets are Creations

Markets are created by entrepreneurs and businesses. Markets are not discovered. They are not found.

In fact, there may not be a "market" per se. The market may be just beginning to form, just developing. It may be new and unfolding. It is in flux, not determined. As such, there is significant uncertainty.

Since there is a high degree of uncertainty, a fluid strategy may involve a fair amount of opportunism. In other words, the strategy involves looking for and responding to opportunities that are evolving in the market.

An excellent example is the market for the iPod that was created by Apple. Prior to Apple's involvement, there was no market for digital music downloads. A person could not purchase and download a single song. Music was only available on CDs and tapes and records. Apple changed the way that music could be purchased and it also designed the iPod music player.

Apple did not "find" this market. It did not discover it. Apple created this market.

The opportunist always has an open mind. He or she remains flexible enough to solve day-to-day problems but still keeps alert for developing new opportunities. And remember, your opportunities for growth may lie outside of your current industry description.

The next section explores the new business models that will be the paradigms for the future.

Thomas Metz

Part IV. Business Models of the Future

11 THE WORLD IS CHANGING

Traditional industry boundaries are blurring, shifting and disappearing. As the boundaries blur, new paradigms are emerging. The new models are reshaping industries into interconnected ecosystems.

The world is becoming more connected in many ways. People are connecting through mobile apps and communities and rewards programs of various kinds. Businesses are focused on giving customers a full experience or solving an overall problem rather than simply selling them a product or a narrow service.

Almost every business is now in the software business in some way. Everything is getting "smart" — like the smart refrigerator that takes a photo every time you shut the refrigerator door. So, when you are at the grocery store you can look at your phone to see if you have eggs.

The Shift to Services
Our economy has been transforming into a more sophisticated economy. As a result, service businesses are playing an increasingly important role. As countries become richer, services sectors become a more prominent part of their economies.

The shift to services is really about selling meaningful outcomes and results. Instead of selling tools, companies need to utilize their tools to provide services to their customers. The relationship with the customer is paramount. The move to services is also being propelled by the ecosystem model.

Services are an excellent way to add new growth areas to a company's business. Many manufacturers have added new services as a way to increase revenues and expand their presence deeper into their markets.

Caterpillar is an good example of a company that is expanding its services business. The company typically experiences cycles of boom and bust because its business is associated with the business cycles of the building and commodity industries. By connecting its machines to the cloud, Caterpillar can troubleshoot remotely and alert customers when they need a new part, a new tire, a tune up or have some other maintenance problem. Selling additional parts and repairs will reduce some of the cyclicality of Caterpillar's business. The company is also selling service agreements similar to those sold by car dealers and manufacturers.

Apple's services business is the fastest growing

segment of its business. These services include iTunes, the App store, Apple Pay, iCloud storage, other internet services and licensing. Service revenues have been increasing and now account for 15% of Apple's revenues. The company's goal is to double it to 30% by 2020. Services are a more consistent revenue stream compared to selling iPhones—an additional benefit.

Another example of a move into services is a truck manufacturing company that was seeking new areas for growth. It acquired a company that provided truck driver training and education. Both firms serve the same set of customers—companies that own trucks. The manufacturer can now sell truck driver training to its existing customers. This acquisition was about providing additional services to customers, not simply trying to sell more trucks.

Another advantage of selling services is that the revenues are often recurring. They are not just one-time sales. This is an excellent side benefit from selling services.

The next chapter discusses how business models are evolving, including recurring revenues, innovative pricing methodologies and changes in the workforce.

12 MODELS ARE CHANGING

A business model describes how a company creates and delivers value for its customers. It defines the value proposition and describes how the company organizes itself in order to produce value.

Since the world is always changing, businesses must continually figure out new ways to deliver value to their customers. How will companies deliver value in the future?

New technologies produce new products and services but they also change the way that products and services are delivered. Thus, the nature of the market changes. When the nature of a market changes, companies must alter their business models. The firms of the future will need to devise business models that are strategically nimble.

Established business models are under assault. They are becoming subject to rapid displacement, disruption, and in some cases, outright destruction. Your business model must adapt to the changing world. The business model that got you there will not be your business model for the future.

Risk averse companies will have a difficult time adapting new business models. You cannot be resistant to change. You cannot just pedal faster. A company does not grow with risk averse behavior. The successful firms are continuously refining their business models.

Strategies must be flexible. Business models need to be more agile and adaptive. This means developing new skills, new processes, new products and whole new ways of working. Build a strong feedback loop with your customers in order to keep ahead of change. Customer expectations and needs can change quickly.

Crafting a new business model means rethinking the value proposition. We are not talking about a minor tweak or a little tinkering, but a more dramatic change. By the way, a new technology does not necessarily alter the business model. Change should be built into your model.

Markets and technologies are moving too fast for a static model. Companies must continually assess and adjust their business models to stay competitive.

Delta Airlines is an example of a company that developed ancillary services to bring in new revenue streams. The company revised its business model in two interesting ways. The Delta TechOps division opened a new jet engine repair facility near Atlanta. It will maintain and repair Rolls-Royce engines for other airlines in addition to its own Delta Airlines planes.

Delta also made a profitable move into the credit card business; it partnered with American Express to introduce a co-branded card. So far, the card has been a big success securing more than one million new accounts and generating $3 billion in revenue in its second year. Delta has done a good job of refashioning its business model.

OPPORTUNITY DRIVES THE BUSINESS MODEL

Since the purpose of the business is to provide value to the customers, customers should drive the business model. Whatever model provides value most effectively is the right model. It is driven by the customer and addressing the customer's needs.

As Peter Drucker expressed:

> It is the customer who determines what a business is. For it is the customer, and he alone, whose willingness to pay for a good or a service converts economic resources into wealth, things into goods. What the business thinks it produces is not of first importance – especially not to the future of the business and to its success. What the customer thinks he or she is buying, what he or she considers "value" is decisive – it determines what a business is, what it produces and whether it will prosper.

(Drucker, Peter. *The Practice of Management.* New York: Harper, 1954, p. 37)

As we discussed earlier in this book, the key to success is to be a customer-centric business. This will drive the successful business models of the future.

There is a straightforward logic that connects business models and opportunity:

Q: Where does growth come from?
A: Growth comes from capitalizing on new opportunities.

Q: Where do new opportunities come from?
A: New opportunities come from the new and changing needs of customers.
Q: How do we solve these new customer problems?
A: First, we must be *aware* of these needs; that's why staying close to the customer is vital.
Second, how we figure out how to solve these problems in *the most effective way*. This way becomes our new business model. It may take some trial and error to get it right, but when we do figure it out, that becomes our new business model.

Thus, the key to growth is solving the customers' new problems. The business model is forged by responding appropriately to opportunities.

The strategy that asks: "How can we sell more widgets" is fine in the short term, but it is not a viable strategy over the long term. What do you do after everyone has enough widgets? Then what? To be successful over the long term a business must do one thing and one thing only — solve your customer's problems. These problems are your opportunities.

Next we examine some of the changes that are occurring in business models.

NEW PARADIGMS FOR REVENUES AND PRICING

Two noteworthy shifts in business models are recurring revenues and innovative pricing paradigms.

Recurring revenues are becoming increasingly important. The first question that I am asked when talking to a potential buyer about acquiring one of my client companies is: "What are the revenues?" The second question is: "What portion of those are recurring?"

Two fundamental points about recurring revenues are significant. First, recurring revenues are less risky. These revenues are more likely to be there next year and the year after that. The second point is that when a company is providing a service and generating recurring revenues, it means that the company has a closer relationship with the customer than to a customer who simply purchased its products. As we discussed earlier, staying close to your customers is a key to long-term success.

Innovative pricing models are emerging. Examples include dynamic pricing, usage-based pricing and the subscription model.

The subscription model is becoming more popular as the world moves from products to services. It goes beyond just one interaction. This model implies an ongoing relationship with the customer.

Volvo has been experimenting with an interesting subscription model for cars. The company charges a simple monthly fee that covers everything except for gas. Unlike a typical lease payment, taxes and insurance are included and you can upgrade to a new car in as few as 24 months. Volvo benefits because the subscription generates closer ties with its customers. Ford is experimenting with a similar subscription model.

The subscription model gives companies valuable information about the behavior of their customers. Volvo gains rich data about the driving habits and preferences of its customers. Companies use this information to develop better and more closely tailored solutions.

Dynamic pricing is another novel pricing model.

Dynamic pricing means that the price changes depending on the level of demand, the time of day or other factors. Companies change their prices to match supply and demand, often in real time. More and more companies are pricing dynamically using machine learning and artificial intelligence. For example, you may pay more for a ride from Uber or Lyft right after the football game is over. Airlines and hotels have used dynamic pricing for years, but now it is becoming common in many industries.

Dynamic pricing, also called adaptive pricing or real-time pricing, is becoming more prevalent in the digital marketplace. Online retailers use dynamic pricing to adjust the price while people are online visiting the retailer's website. A shopper may be one click away from leaving the site; dynamic pricing enables the retailer to make a real-time price adjustment and improve conversion rates.

Pricing based on usage is also becoming more common. Paying for cloud storage services on Microsoft Azure or Amazon Web Services is an example of usage-based pricing. Twilio is another example of usage pricing. Twilio enables app developers to include special features — such as audio, video and text communication — in their apps. The company charges a small amount for each message sent.

Companies will have to learn how to reduce the complexity of systems and operations. Many business operations will become more project oriented. Training will become a more important competency.

A company's relationship with its employees and workforce will change. Businesses will need to reinvent their workforce and look beyond their organizational boundaries. Companies will have to learn how to manage a distributed workforce.

Freelance will be more prevalent in the future. As more people become freelancers, the workforce will become more liquid. Companies will use on-demand platforms to explore the open talent market. This offers much more flexibility, both for the company and for the worker.

Next we examine how ecosystems and platforms can impact your business in a positive way.

Thomas Metz

13 ECOSYSTEMS AND PLATFORMS

B usiness ecosystems are all the talk these days. The ecosystem paradigm is becoming increasingly prevalent. The model is compelling new types of interactions and relationships among businesses.

WHAT IS AN ECOSYTEM?

The term ecosystem is used in biology to describe a community of organisms that interact in their environment. A business ecosystem operates in a similar manner. A business ecosystem is a dynamic network of companies that interact with each other in a variety of ways. Their purpose is to create value, exchange products and services, collaborate, share information and generally support each other.

The ecosystem paradigm is important because it compels new types of relationships and interactions among the players. Ecosystems are not new, but they are becoming increasingly prevalent and important. New digital ecosystems are transforming the way that organizations deliver value. These new ecosystems drive strategies and enable new business models.

In an ecosystem a variety of parties find new ways to interact for mutual benefit. There are multiple connections and relationships with the different players. The relationship between the businesses is what matters.

Kohl's department stores is a good example of a company participating in an ecosystem. Kohl's has 1,150 stores across 49 states. Kohl's has partnered with Amazon. It allows people to return items to a Kohl's store that were purchased at Amazon. About 100 stores have this capability so far. This makes the return process extremely easy for Amazon customers. In addition, 30 Kohl's stores showcase some Amazon electronic products like the Echo. It is a good arrangement—both companies benefit and the consumers benefit as well.

An ecosystem is dynamic, not static. This means that it is different from a network or an association. The parties *interact* with each other, typically on an ongoing basis.

Success depends on taking customers on the best possible journeys. This is something that few businesses will be able to accomplish alone; they will need to be part of an ecosystem. The world of ecosystems is a more customer-centric model. Users are enjoying a more in-depth experience and they can choose from wider array of products and services through a single access point.

Many companies are participating in more than just a single ecosystem—sometimes several, often overlapping ecosystems. Occasionally, the ecosystems are multidimensional.

A good example of a company attempting to gain a stronger position in its ecosystem is Broadcom, a manufacturer of semiconductor chips for smartphones and computers. The company develops software that supports its chips, but software is only a small part of its business. Broadcom acquired CA Technologies, a large developer of software for enterprise management and mainframe computers.

The strategic rationale is to help Broadcom become a stronger player as an infrastructure technology company, that includes both hardware and software. The acquisition enables Broadcom to expand into a whole new area. Management views this acquisition as a natural extension of the ecosystem in which they are participating.

The challenge is to figure out how your business fits into the ecosystem. How can you take advantage of the nature of the ecosystem? Your competitive advantage will depend on the strength of the partners and ecosystems that you build.

If you view your company and your markets as part of an ecosystem, it can change the way that you think about your strategy going forward. It influences your thinking about the types of opportunities to pursue.

THE PLATFORM PARADIGM

The platform paradigm underlies the ecosystem. Companies aggregate their services into a single convenient point of access — the platform.

Platform-based ecosystems are the new plane of competition. The platform provides the marketplace infrastructure that brings together producers and consumers. Airbnb is a platform. eBay is a platform. Amazon is a platform.

The key is to build a platform that will reshape and optimize the way that your products and services are conceived, produced and delivered. Companies do not necessarily own the products or services that are sold on the platform. For example, Apple's App Store sells apps that it does not own.

Uber is the quintessential example of a successful platform. The Uber platform handles the multitude of tasks for getting a ride simply and easily. A few taps on your phone and you are on your way. Easy peasy.

Remember the old way of catching a taxi cab? Find their phone number. Call the company. Tell them where you are. Wonder when the cab will actually show up — it could be a short or long time. Take the ride and hope the cabbie does not get lost or take the long route. Pay with cash or with a credit card. Paying with a card was a bit of bother. Ask for a receipt. Easy peasy? No, not in the slightest.

The Uber platform automatically handles all aspects, making the experience as easy as possible for the customers. And, in my experience, the cars are cleaner and the drivers are more interesting to talk to. A thought-provoking side note — Uber never could have existed in 2008.

Every platform is a community and the players in the community can be leveraged. As the platform grows, the number of interactions among the players escalates. This increases the competitive advantage of the platform.

The platform enables companies to interact with their customers in new and richer ways. As a result, the customer relationship is changing. Each customer interaction will become more personalized, natural and powerful.

Every company will need a platform strategy. Companies can build their own platforms or participate in the platforms and ecosystems of other players. The fundamental point is that platforms and ecosystems are successful is because they offer a fuller and richer experience for the customer.

Thomas Metz

Part V. Best Practices — The Discipline of Company Definition

14 CONSTRUCT A FIRST-RATE DEFINITION

A well-crafted company definition includes several key components. Four simple rules set the stage for creating a top-notch definition:

1. State the problem that you solve for the customer.
2. State who your customers are and the markets that you serve.
3. Skip the fluff, the nonsense and the BS.
4. Make sure that it is dead clear how you deliver value to your customers.

A good company definition can include creative and artistic phraseology. It does not have to sound like it is generated by a computer. The four rules above are guidelines; they leave a lot of room for creative interpretation. Remember that the most important thing is that the reader clearly understands what the company is about. That is the destination and there are many paths to get there.

This is an excellent definition:

> *Mattersight unleashes the power of personality to improve every interaction with every customer every time. With tools to learn, analyze, and predict customer behavior based on customer conversations, Mattersight helps brands create chemistry with their customers through shorter, more satisfying conversations that increase loyalty.* (www.mattersight.com)

The definition states the problem that the firm solves and how the customer benefits. The customers are stated simply, as brands. It uses no buzzwords and it is actually kind of fun to read. Nice job. (Mattersight was acquired in 2018 by NICE Ltd., a provider of analytics software.)

A powerful definition is clear. The reader does not have doubts about what the company is, who it serves or how it adds value. It is dead clear.

What the Definition is *Not*

A company definition is not a mission statement or a vision statement. These statements are often vague, fluffy and devoid of meaning. A solid company definition is much more important than a nebulous mission or vision statement. A definition is real. It characterizes who you are.

GOOD DEFINITIONS

Before we delve into the guidelines for constructing a first-rate company definition, let's take a look at a few examples of really good definitions.

The definition of Digital River is quite good:

> *With nearly 25 years of industry experience, Digital River has mastered the ins and outs of global ecommerce. The company specializes in taking high-tech brands direct to their customers, whether they live around the corner or around the world.*
>
> *Leading software and services, consumer electronics and digital game brands rely on Digital River's advanced commerce cloud, monetization tools and global ecommerce solutions to market and sell their products online. From start to finish, Digital River makes it easy to manage storefronts, take orders, process payments, automate subscriptions and drive delivery. At the same time, the company works behind the scenes to handle fraud, billing, taxes and compliance, so businesses and consumers can shop with confidence and peace of mind.* ("Digital River Appoints Adam Coyle." 10 July 2018, www.digitalriver.com/our-company/newsroom/press-release/digital-river-appoints-adam-coyle-chief-executive-officer.)

Although a little too long, this definition is quite good. The first paragraph is vague and not particularly helpful, but then the definition hits the mark. It tells you exactly what the company does for the customer. It mentions the market and the types of companies that are its customers. It describes the solutions that it sells and what these solutions are used for (marketing and selling products online). The definition goes on to explain the tasks that the customers can accomplish (problems that it solves). The reader will have a very clear understanding of how Digital River delivers value to its customers.

Another good definition is that of Descartes.

Descartes (Nasdaq:DSGX) (TSX:DSG) is the global leader in providing on-demand, software-as-a-service solutions focused on improving the productivity, performance and security of logistics-intensive businesses. Customers use our modular, software-as-a-service solutions to route, schedule, track and measure delivery resources; plan, allocate and execute shipments; rate, audit and pay transportation invoices; access global trade data; file customs and security documents for imports and exports; and complete numerous other logistics processes by participating in the world's largest, collaborative multimodal logistics community. ("Descartes Acquires STEPcom." 27 June 2019, www.descartes.com/news-events/general-news/descartes-acquires-stepcom.)

This is a good definition. It states specifically who their customers are — logistics-intensive businesses. It goes on to state exactly how customers utilize the solutions in their businesses. There are a few buzzwords, long lists and awkward phrases but other than that, this is an excellent definition. Anyone reading this definition will have absolutely no doubt about who the customers are, what the company does and how it delivers value to its customers.

Let's review one more so that you really get the idea.

> *Determine, a Corcentric company, is a leading global provider of SaaS Source-to-Pay and Enterprise Contract Lifecycle Management (ECLM) solutions. The Determine Cloud Platform provides procurement, legal and finance professionals analytics of their supplier, contract and financial performance. Our technologies empower customers to drive new revenue, identify savings, improve compliance and mitigate risk.* (www.determine.com.)

We could do without the "leading global provider," that provides exactly zero information to the reader. This is one of the most overused phrases in the world of company definitions. But then the definition gets good. It succinctly states the type of customers that it serves and the value that it provides to these customers. The last sentence spells out the specific benefits that the customer receives. Note that these benefits are not vague phrases like "be more profitable," but benefits specific to the use of their services. This is an excellent definition.

TRAPS TO AVOID

There are a few simple traps to avoid to improve the quality of your definition. Try not to use buzzwords; they are unconvincing. Skip the superlatives. Avoid cute phrases, fluff and BS. They do not add anything and you would be surprised at how prevalent they are. Do not include long lists and do not try to set a new record for the world's longest sentence.

Buzzwords are not Powerful

Buzzwords are weak, very weak. They are the exact opposite of clear communication. One's eyes glaze over when reading meaningless buzzwords over and over again. There is no reason ever to use buzzwords. They convey no meaning. There are 650,000 words in English language. Try using a different word. You have plenty to choose from.

Buzzwords and cute phrases proliferate company definitions. For example:

leading global provider — This is an empty phrase.

innovative — Everyone says they are innovative. This is like saying "easy to use" which has been a cliché for decades.

deep — This is the most overused word in the technology universe. Ugh!

drive disruption — Yes, very cool. Very trendy.

drive rapid growth — "Drive" is so hackneyed. Get yourself a new word.

purpose-built — What the heck is "purpose-built"? As, opposed to what? Accidentally built?

omnichannel solutions — Maybe you know what that is but it sounds phony.

in a digital world — Give me a break. What part of the world is not digital these days?

More buzzwords:
technology-enabled
holistic
global deployments
omnichannel engagement
digital workplace solutions
innovative collaboration solutions
data-driven digital transformation
a prime vector for growth

If you can't describe your company without using buzzwords, you have a problem.

Skip the Superlatives
Superlatives make one's eyes glaze over, for example:
best of breed
best in class
award-winning
industry-leading solutions
world-class company

Cute and Meaningless Phrases
Cute phrases abound in company definitions. A few examples:

Driving mission critical business processes
— Total fluff.

For the world's leading and emerging companies
— Impressive!

A global performance improvement solutions provider
— Excuse me?

With a vision to help maximize the potential of people through technology.
     — This is completely devoid of meaning.

We're on a mission to help our customers capitalize on new opportunities in the connected world.
     — I'm glad we are clear on that.

A profitable and growing technology leader headquartered in …
     — Jeesh!

Discard the cute phrases. They obstruct clear communication.

Fluff and BS

Fluff and BS are not effective communication. Fluff just gets in the way. What do we mean by fluff and BS? Here are a few examples.

The Company provides the design assets, technology and expertise that help create beautiful, authentic and impactful brands that customers will engage with and value, wherever they experience the brand, now and in the future.

The Company empowers digital leaders to easily create standout experiences for customers — everywhere they engage, and always with measurable business results.

     — These paragraphs mean absolutely nothing.

With a commitment to deliver industry-leading

products, knowledge, solutions, and customer service.
— Everyone says that.

Services to world-class companies to help them achieve mission-critical objectives, lower costs, improve agility and increase competitive advantages.

> — This is a totally meaningless sentence. Are they just trying to sound cool? Who would write a sentence like that?

The Company develops and fields transformative, affordable technology, platforms and systems for United States National Security related customers, allies and commercial enterprises.
— Huh?

The Company enables companies to fuel innovation, become more agile and realize new growth opportunities, resulting in intelligent market disruptions.
— Totally meaningless.

Do not put minutia up front, like where you are located or how many people you employ. This is not critical information. You can include it later, if at all.

No Laundry Lists
A "laundry list" is a list of many terms, one after another. These types of lists do not communicate effectively. They are actually quite weak. Why do so many firms include laundry lists? Because they are so easy. You just list one thing after another; no thinking is required.

For example: "designs, develops, produces and markets..." Almost every business does those things. Those words are not informative.

Another example of a laundry list:

Specializing in infrastructure, cloud, security, applications, collaboration and big data & analytics solutions, as well as rack integration services and first call support.

— This is a long list of stuff, all nouns and no verbs. Verbs are actually helpful in sentences.

The system includes accounting, cash management, purchasing, vendor management, financial consolidation, revenue recognition, subscription billing, contract management, project accounting, fund accounting, inventory management, and financial reporting applications

Can't they summarize these product areas into something with fewer words? Those things may all be true, but this is not a good way to communicate what the company is about. It would be more effective to group some of these items. It would also be helpful to mention the customer's problem.

A fully-integrated platform, flexible benefits and compliance administration, HR consulting, and time and labor management as well as a full suite of workspace management solutions for conference room scheduling, desk sharing programs, and real estate optimization.

Long lists of words and phrases like this are probably the worst way to communicate. One final example of a laundry list...I am getting a headache:

> *Our premise, cloud, and innovative premise/cloud hybrid platforms include ACD, predictive dialing, blended processing, recording and monitoring, IVR, messaging, interaction analytics, decisioning, and workforce management.*

Multiple Lists in One Sentence

List are not good in the first place, but having multiple lists in one sentence is really bad. This one sentence includes three lists:

> *The Company is a leading provider of information technology and engineering services that include data analytics, agile development, mobility, training, and cyber security solutions to the intelligence, defense, homeland security, and federal civilian markets.*

Let's parse this sentence. The company provides two services and five solutions to four markets...all in only *one* sentence. Talk about hard to read and hard to understand. Sure, it is technically accurate but it is extremely difficult to grasp. Unfortunately, this is how many company definitions are crafted.

The corollary to this rule is: One sentence, one point. You are not writing a novel. Each sentence should convey one and only one idea. Too many definitions try to pack two or three and sometimes four completely different points into one sentence. This makes for rough reading and poor communication. You want your readers to get it. The best way to do that is to convey only one point per sentence.

Do not use multiple modifiers. Multiple modifiers are three or four or even five words all modifying one noun. Consider this example, talk about a mouthful, this is several mouths full.

The Company's comprehensive content, business, advertising, and experience management solutions.

That phrase includes five modifiers for the word "solutions!" One more example:

The Company's cloud-based marketing data quality automation solutions.

Are People Afraid of Periods?
Long sentences do not make for good communication. In fact, they make it difficult for the reader to get the gist. Why not simply insert a period and then start a new sentence? It's not hard to do. There must be fear of periods. Would that be called periodaphobia?

Driving mission critical business processes such as configure, price and quote, contract and rebate management, business intelligence, and regulatory compliance, the Company's solutions transform the revenue lifecycle from a series of disjointed operations into a strategic end-to-end process.

That is 40 words in one sentence! Amazing. Surely, there a shortage of periods. Why not break it up into three sentences and make it absolutely clear? Periods are free. One more example:

As the industry rapidly evolves to meet the "anytime, anywhere" demands of today's viewers, the Company's comprehensive content, business, advertising, and experience management solutions provide a mature, network-agnostic, cloud-enabled platform of scalable core capabilities that video service providers, broadcasters, content owners and brand advertisers need to create the personalized, individual experiences that drive viewer engagement and monetization.

A 57-word sentence! Call the Guinness Book! This writer is clearly afraid of the dreaded period.

I wonder what the writer of this sentence was thinking. Perhaps he or she believes that once a person starts to read the sentence that the reader is hooked. In other words, they can't stop reading; they cannot get out of the sentence! This, of course, is ridiculous. Even if they finished the whole damn sentence, they would have no idea what it means. Get real. Get some periods!

This chapter illustrated some of the common traps that should be avoided in order to construct an effective company definition. Too many company definitions in the technology world are similar to these examples. They are full of fluff and BS and devoid of meaning.

Crafting an intelligent definition is not really that difficult. Simply make it dead clear what you do. Why does your business exist? What problem do you solve for your customers? Do not obsess about your products or your cool technology. Just make it clear how you serve your customers.

15 CRITIQUE OF POOR DEFINITIONS

In this chapter we review several mediocre definitions and then examine a number of definitions that are really quite poor. Critiquing the poor definitions makes it very obvious what to do and what not to do when trying to craft an excellent company definition.

Remember the basic premise — that a business exists to create and deliver value to its customers. That is the sole reason for its existence. The company definition must reflect this principle. The definition should state the problem that it solves for its customers and who the customers are.

First of all, how do we judge whether a definition is good, bad or mediocre? Part of the research for this book included reviewing the definitions of companies in technology-related markets. My judgments are certainly qualitative and subjective. I found it helpful to ask several questions when reviewing the definitions.

The questions were:

- Is it clear how the company helps its customers?
- Is it clear who the customers are?
- Is it clear what market the company is participating in?
- After reading the definition, do I understand why the company exists?

Bad company definitions make me cranky. I vacillated between writing this chapter with detached professionalism or rather not so professionally with a little attitude. I opted to go with attitude. First of all, reading a critique that contains attitude is more fun. (What could be more fun than reading about company definitions?) So, a smidgen attitude will make it a little less boring. Secondly, I have attitude. Thus, in the spirit of honest appraisal, I am critiquing these definitions with more than just a little attitude.

Before we dig into the poor definitions, let's examine a few of the most common definitions — the mediocre ones.

MEDIOCRE DEFINITIONS

These pedestrian definitions characteristically convey information about products and technology. They do not mention how the products help the customer. Plus, the market descriptions are overly broad.

These typical definitions are not terrible, but they are not good either. They are not exactly punchy and hard-hitting. More importantly, a person would not read the definition and then say — "Oh yes, I know exactly what this company does."

Let's consider a few mediocre definitions:

> *Bel (www.belfuse.com) designs, manufactures and markets a broad array of products that power, protect and connect electronic circuits. These products are primarily used in the networking, telecommunications, computing, military and aerospace, transportation and broadcasting industries.*
>
> *Bel's product groups include Magnetic Solutions (integrated connector modules, power transformers, power inductors and discrete components), Power Solutions and Protection (front-end, board-mount and industrial power products, module products and circuit protection) and Connectivity Solutions (expanded beam fiber optic, copper-based, RF and RJ connectors and cable assemblies). The Company operates facilities around the world.* ("Bel Announces USB 2.0 Combination MagJack ICMs." 16 Jan. 2019, belfuse.com/news-detail/bel-announces-usb-2-0-combination-magjack-icms.)

Bel's definition is a typical self-focused technology definition. The definition does mention seven industries that it participates in. But these industries are so broad that the sentence describing them has little meaning. The next paragraph is one very long sentence and it cites three product groups and then lists the products sold by each group. This definition is basically a list of products and a broad statement of its markets. There is no mention of the customers. It does obliquely refer to the problems it solves in the first sentence — products that power, protect and connect electronic circuits. So that part is good.

Let's critique another mediocre definition:

Better software means better projects. Deltek is the leading global provider of enterprise software and information solutions for project-based businesses. More than 23,000 organizations and millions of users in over 80 countries around the world rely on Deltek for superior levels of project intelligence, management and collaboration. Our industry-focused expertise powers project success by helping firms achieve performance that maximizes productivity and revenue. ("Deltek and Grant Thornton Form Alliance." 14 Feb. 2019, www.deltek.com/en/about/media-center/press-releases/2019/deltek-and-grant-thornton-form-alliance.)

Okay, we could do without the "leading global provider" because that tells us nothing. The market description is broad but not too bad; it does mention "project-based businesses" which is a good description of the types of companies that use its services. The number of users and organizations does not help the reader understand what the company does, but it sounds somewhat impressive.

It does point out that their software helps with projects which is good. But the word choice is awkward. "Industry focused expertise" is a meaningless expression. The phrase "achieve performance that maximizes productivity and revenue" is okay, but it does not really drive the point home. This definition is mediocre at best.

POOR DEFINITIONS

Examples of bad definitions are actually much more

helpful for guiding people to build a first-rate company definition. It is easy to point out what *not* to do.

Fluff and Vagueness

This is a good example of fluff and vagueness. We have disguised the company names to avoid embarrassing the firms.

> *The Company, headquartered in City, State, offers intuitive and innovative solutions designed to help organizations of all sizes and complexities build companies of the future. Our cloud platforms enable more than xx,000 clients worldwide to better manage their people and space in a mobile, digital, multi-generational, and global workplace. The Company's offerings include a fully-integrated platform, flexible benefits and compliance administration, consulting, and time and labor management as well as a full suite of workspace management solutions for scheduling, desk sharing programs, and real estate optimization.*

The first two sentences tell us exactly nothing about the company—they are completely meaningless. The definition includes a litany of buzzwords: innovative, intuitive, "build companies of the future," "multigenerational and global workplace," "fully integrated." After reading this so-called definition, one has absolutely no idea of what the company does, who its customers are and what problems the company solves. It has something to do with benefits and compliance but that's about all we know.

Let's consider another example:

> *The Company provides global organizations with a*

*modern approach to Digital Transformation to succeed
in the Information Economy. The Company is the only
solutions provider for both Information Management
and IT Systems. The Company's Information
Management solutions enable companies to find,
understand, govern and deliver information of any
kind, from any source — whether structured or
unstructured — through its lifecycle from capture to
analysis to consumption.*

This definition is almost totally meaningless. The
sentences may be true but they do not convey any useful
knowledge to the reader. It is complete fluff.

One more example:

*The Company designs, develops, produces and markets
innovative products, systems and services for
advanced communications solutions. The Company
sells products to a diverse customer base in the global
commercial and government communications markets.*

This could be almost anything. It is totally vague.
Once again, it communicates nothing real or helpful to
the reader. There is no mention of who the customers
are. The words are almost devoid of meaning.

One final example:

*The Company is an international multi-skilled
solution provider providing digital enablement
services to help customers harness digital technology
and innovative services to deliver powerful business
outcomes.*

— Any questions?

Do People Really Talk Like That?

What if the customer talked like that? Could you imagine what it would sound like if the customer used similar language? If you asked a real customer why they worked with a particular company, would the customer say:

> *"We use Acme Corp. because they are a leading global provider of..."*

Of course not. People just don't talk like that. They would never use the words "leading global provider." Would they say the following?

> *"We use Acme Corp. because they design, develop, produce and market innovative products systems and services for advanced communication solutions?"*

What do you think? Do you talk like that? Of course not! Human beings simply do not talk like that.

How might a customer actually talk? Customers would speak more simply and they would describe the company in terms of how it helps them solve their problems. This is how a real customer might actually talk:

> *We use Acme Corp. because they solve our xyz problem quickly and effectively. Their people know what they are doing. Plus, their prices are pretty good.*

That is how human beings talk.

What if you asked your customers what your

company does? How would they answer that question? Would they say "We use Acme Corp. because they are technology enabled?" Would they say "We like Acme Corp. because they have a purpose-built platform?" Would they use the term "holistic"? No, they would not. Human beings do not talk like that.

If your definition was read out loud by a customer, would it sound the least bit plausible or would it sound ridiculous? That is a good clue to recognize whether or not your definition is on the mark.

The next chapter encapsulates 16 rules to construct a really good definition.

16 SIXTEEN RULES FOR A GREAT COMPANY DEFINITION

We discussed the guidelines for crafting a great company definition at some length in Chapter 14. It might be helpful to specify these rules in one place for easy reference. So here they are.

Six Positive Rules

First let's review the positive rules, things to absolutely remember as you craft your definition.

1. Clearly express the problem that you solve for your customer.
2. State what types of companies are your customers.
3. State very simply the markets that you serve.
4. Make it clear how you deliver value. There is more room for creativity with this one, but make it clear.

5. One sentence — one point. Each sentence should communicate one and only one point. This may be a little boring but you are not writing a novel. One sentence, one point makes it clear and easy for the reader.
6. Keep it simple. There is clarity in simplicity.

The Do Nots

Now for the negative rules. Below are ten bad habits to avoid at all costs when constructing your definition. It is not difficult to follow these rules. Just do it.

7. No buzzwords.
8. Skip the superlatives.
9. No meaningless or hackneyed phrases.
10. No fluff or BS.
11. No laundry lists.
12. No multiple lists in one sentence.
13. No vague or rambling phrases.
14. No multiple modifiers. Do not use three, four or five adjectives to modify a noun. This is cumbersome and a waste of good words.
15. No long sentences.
16. No minutia up front, like where you are located or how many employees you have. This is not critical information.

APPENDIX A: THE RESEARCH BEHIND THE BOOK

The research behind this book originated from two sources. The first source is my investment banking experience. Over several decades, I have examined many thousands of websites with the question in mind — would this company be a good potential buyer for the company that I am selling?

Where does one find company definitions? The two primary sources of company definition are: (1) the company's website and (2) at the end of the company's press releases. Website descriptions vary all over the place. Much of the information is sales and marketing oriented. Sometimes it is simply a description of products and services. These sales-oriented descriptions do not define the company in any meaningful way.

To find a more precise definition, the best place to look is at the bottom of the company's press releases. Most companies issue press releases periodically describing new products, recent events, executive changes or other happenings at the company. At the end of every press release is the company description.

The second source of information about company definition resulted from research that I undertook to substantiate my ideas for this book. I reviewed the definitions of 350 technology, software and tech-related companies. About 200 firms were midsized companies with revenues from $25 million to $500 million and 150 were large companies with revenues greater than $500 million. These are technology companies in the broad sense. They include software companies, hardware companies, service companies and some are a combination.

I posed several questions to facilitate making sound judgments about the definitions. The questions were:

- Is it clear how the company helps its customers?
- Is it clear who the customers are?
- Is it clear what market the company is participating in?
- After reading the definition, do I understand why the company exists?

The challenge was to figure out a standard way to judge the definitions so that it would be relatively clear whether the definitions were good, or not so good, and why.

Rating the Definitions

In reviewing the definitions, I needed a method to make reasonable judgments about the quality of the definitions. I developed a rating system to determine the effectiveness of the definitions. The system is not scientific and is certainly more qualitative than quantitative. But it was a reasonable method for making judgments about the definitions.

On the rating scale, 10 was excellent and 1 was quite bad. If I got a slight headache reading the definition, then I would rate the definition at most a 4 and perhaps worse.

The definition rating scale:
1. Bad
2. Very poor
3. Poor
4. Poorish
5. Mediocre
6. Okay, so-so
7. Okay, it has a good point or two
8. Pretty good
9. Very good
10. Excellent

Several conclusions materialized from reviewing the 350 definitions. The first conclusion was a subtle one, but eventually a picture began to develop. About 75% of the company definitions were not particularly clear at all. They included buzzwords, fancy phrases and trendy jargon. They were trying to sound cool. There was little emphasis on describing who the customers were and what problems they solved for the customers.

Yes, many of the definitions were technically accurate. However, they were vague. Vague to the point of meaninglessness. This was not good communication.

Summary of the ratings:

Bad to somewhat poor	60%
Mediocre	15%
Okay to very good	25%

It was fairly easy to discern whether the writer was trying to use buzzwords and cool sounding phrases to feed you a bunch of BS or whether they are actually trying to help you understand what the company was about.

The Window into Strategy

The second part of the book discusses growth strategy and opportunity. For three decades I have arranged the sales of companies in the technology, software and tech-service industries. Almost all of these transactions were strategic in nature. The buyer saw a strategic advantage in making the acquisition. The buyer acquired new technology, new software, a new business model or some other unique asset that was strategically important.

As a result of participating in these strategic acquisitions, I developed an appreciation for how companies consider their growth strategies, acquisitions and new opportunities. My remarks on strategy derive from this viewpoint into growth strategy.

ABOUT THE AUTHOR

Thomas V. Metz, Jr. founded the boutique investment bank T.V. Metz & Co., LLC in 1983. The primary focus is arranging the sale of companies in which value is strategic, typically in the technology, software and tech-service industries. Mr. Metz has closed transactions across North America as well as Europe and Asia.

Earlier he invested venture capital for Gramark, a private holding company. He held positions in finance with the DeLorean Motor Company and computer sales with IBM.

Mr. Metz holds a degree in Mathematics and Computer Science from the University of Oregon. He earned an MBA degree from the University of California at Berkeley. He is a frequent speaker on mergers, acquisitions and entrepreneurial topics.

He has authored three other books: *Selling the Intangible Company — How to Negotiate and Capture the Value of a Growth Firm* (Wiley & Sons, 2009), *Perfect Your Exit Strategy — Seven Steps to Maximum Value* (Bettencourt, 2016) and *Why is the United States Rich? 10 Myths Exposed* (Bettencourt, 2021).

He is an avid golfer and heli-skier. In his younger years he was a top nationally ranked squash player. He also pilots his airplane, a Cessna 182 named Loretta, to family and golf destinations.

INDEX